Contents

KU-013-154

Introduction

Crafts and arts can be uniquely exciting and tremendous fun, but only, it has to be said, if you have a good collection of designs, patterns and motifs for the job in hand. This book provides such a collection.

Containing over 300 patterns and forms, it is a design manual that draws its inspiration from all manner of traditional, folk and tribal crafts. With designs from such primary sources as eighteenth and nineteenth century American textiles, patchworks, quilts and appliqués; from early English illuminated manuscripts; from sixteenth century Russian, Polish and German wood carvings; from eighteenth century black African textiles – and so the list goes on. The contents open up a whole new world of designs, patterns, motifs and forms.

Textiles, ceramics, wood carvings, metal work, graphics, interior design and decoration – each has its own characteristic joys, challenges and rewards. To work a delicate embroidery with fine silks; to use a smooth, soft, long haired brush to pick out slipwork design on a piece of pottery; to use a razor-shaped gouge to carve a clean and crisp motif on a piece of wood; to weave; to print; to knit; to make jewellery; to stencil – this book will help you realise and achieve your own ambitions.

To be able to draw inspiration from a tried and trusted traditional design source and then to spend all your available time at an art or craft – wonderful! Then to stand back and to know that the object created has been worked with your own two hands – these are truly pleasuresome, exhilarating fingertingling experiences that should not be missed. There need be no more aimless searching around for a new pattern and no more worrying because your particular creative experience seems to be grinding to a halt, for no other reason than it needs an unusual design or pattern to make it that little bit special. Now you will have quick access to hundreds of beautiful and functional forms, decorations and pattern compositions. And, of course, if and when you do need to search out more designs, this book will show you the way. With each design having a clear and concisely numbered caption to place it in a time and space context, you will have at your fingertips all the clues and leads you need to enable you to hunt down more of the same.

To help you swiftly locate the style you want, each design has been reduced to a common denominator of line and tone, and then redrawn and presented as a co-ordinated image that is both exciting and accessible. Each and every design, pattern and motif has been arranged and grouped according to its underlying form – the line, the circle, entwined patterns, plant forms, animal forms and borders.

No problem if you are in hurry and you need a specific type or character of pattern, design or motif; all you do is home-in on the group or type of pattern structures with which you are most concerned. So, for example, let us say that you are looking for a 'bird' form, or a 'circle', or whatever, all you have to do is refer to the pattern related section and away you go. No more worrying about museum copyright or publishers' permission – the designs are yours!

We offer crafts people, designers and artists quick access to hundreds of beautiful and functional forms, decorations, and pattern compositions. Whether you are looking for inspiration, guidance for an original design, or are trying to duplicate the style of a specific country, folk or tribal form, or period, then you'll find this book an invaluable aid.

Luton Sixth Form College
Library

WITHDRAWN

43515

4.95 745

Traditional
and Folk Designs

Luton Sixth Form College
Library

00023175

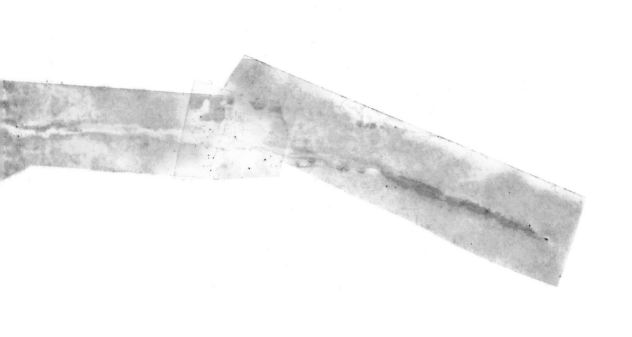

Traditional and Folk Designs

for Embroidery, Painting, Pottery and all other crafts

Alan and Gill Bridgewater

SEARCH PRESS

First published in Great Britain 1990

Search Press Ltd.
Wellwood, North Farm Road,
Tunbridge Wells, Kent TN2 3DR

All rights reserved.
The text and the compilation of the designs in this book,
copyright © Alan and Gill Bridgewater.

A total of twelve illustrations may be reproduced for any
one project, or in any single publication, without written
permission being obtained beforehand from Search Press
Limited.

The reproduction of this book as a whole is prohibited.

ISBN 0 85532 654 9

00023175
43515
745

Typeset by Scribe Design, 123 Watling Street, Gillingham, Kent
Printed in Spain by Elkar S. Coop, Bilbao 12, Spain

1. Russia – textile; woven (nineteenth century)

2. Russia – textile; woven (twentieth century)

3. England – pottery; scratched slip (nineteenth century)

4. Bulgaria – wood; poker work (nineteenth century)

5. Czechoslovakia – pottery; painted (seventeenth century)

6. Germany – pottery; painted and scratched (early eighteenth century)

7. Java – textile; batik (nineteenth century)

8. Sweden – architectural, wall; painting (eighteenth century)

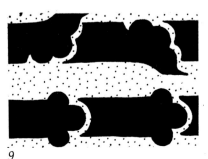

9. France – architectural, wall; stencil printed (fifteenth century?)

10. Russia – pottery; painted (eighteenth century)

Introduction to lines

A line is a narrow, continuous mark that is produced by a moving point. It is a straight or curved continuous trace, having no breadth.

Just about everything can, in its barest most basic essentials, be reduced to line. Give a child a pencil and paper, and ask him to draw a pattern, and he will almost certainly start by building a noughts and crosses grid, or by drawing a zigzag.

Lines set vertically, lines set horizontally and lines set obliquely, even though such linear forms are non-figurative, they have come, by convention, to have special attributes. We think of vertical lines as possessing power and energy, horizonal lines as being calm or having to do with sleep, and oblique lines as suggesting, or being capable of rapid, spring-like movement. This is, of course, not to say that traditional pattern makers –potters, weavers, wood carvers and the like – are necessarily consciously aware that this pattern suggests repose, or that pattern suggests potential energy or movement. Rather, this is how we have come, over the centuries, to interpret such design structures.

Although we know line decoration to be limitless – we only have to look around us to see that this is a fact – when, as craftsmen or designers, we come right down to making and constructing linear decorations, we find ourselves limited by craft context. The techniques influence and shape the form of the design, so that the character of the patterns, designs and motifs are determined by the materials and by the tools. So, for example, when soft plastic clay is combed vertically one type of linear pattern is created; a row of knife cuts on wood produces another; a line of embroidered stitches produces another; rhythmic strokes of a paint-loaded brush produce another – all different, and yet all the same. The craft context produces exciting and subtle variations in pattern, form and emphasis.

Each and every craft process makes its own characteristic marks but, even more exciting, some patterns grow out of the making process, while others are consciously applied. The grooves made by the potter's fingers as he pushes and pulls at a mound of spinning clay are quite different in structure, and character, from the bands of lines made when he rolls a wheel across a soft clay tile.

Grids, squares, bands of vertical lines, zigzags, che boards, counterchanges, chevrons, furrows, diamonds – all are linear designs. Have a good long look through the line section, and see how identical pattern structures can be transformed by variously reversing the tone, by changing the position of the pattern on the ground, or by shifting the emphasis. A black square on a white ground is the same as a white square on black ground – but is it!

1. Africa – textile; woven (nineteenth century)

2. Lithuania – wood; carved and stained (nineteenth century)

3. Africa – textile; printed (nineteenth century)

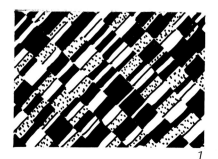

1 *2* *3*

4. *North America – bone; carved (eighteenth century)*

5. *Bulgaria – textile; woven (nineteenth century)*

6. *Bulgaria – textile; woven (nineteenth century)*

7. *Lithuania – wood; incised (nineteenth century)*

8. *Africa – textile; painted (nineteenth century)*

9. *Africa – textile; combed (nineteenth century)*

10. *Africa – wood; carved (nineteenth century)*

11. *Africa – textile; combed (nineteenth century)*

12, *New Guinea – wood; carved and painted (nineteenth century)*

13. *Africa – textile; combed (nineteenth century)*

1. *Persia – pottery; painted (twelfth century)*

2. *England – pottery; slip trailed (seventeenth century)*

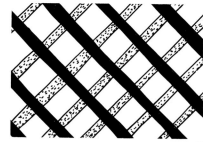

3. *England – book; illuminated (date ?)*

4. *Africa – wood; carved (nineteenth century)*

5. *England – wood; inlay (seventeenth century)*

6. *England – pottery; pierced (eighteenth century)*

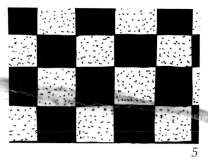

7. *America – textile; woven (nineteenth century)*

8. *Poland – textile; woven (nineteenth century)*

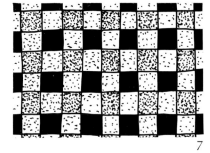

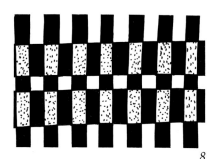

9. *Poland – textile; woven (nineteenth century)*

10. *Africa – wood; carved (fifteenth century)*

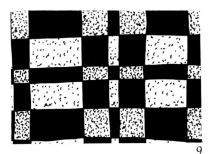

1. *Africa – textile; embroidered (nineteenth century)*

2. *England – pottery; slip painted (seventeenth century)*

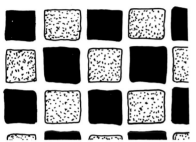

3. *Italy – pottery; incised (4000 BC)*

4. *Africa – textile; printed (twentieth century)*

5. *Persia –pottery; painted (4000 BC)*

6. *Middle East – pottery; painted (4000 BC)*

7. *Africa – metal; cast (pre-fifteenth century)*

8. *Africa – textile; printed (nineteenth century)*

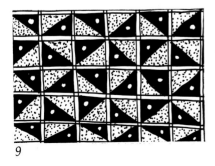

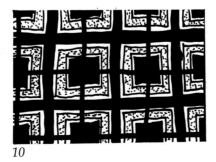

9. *Africa – textile; printed (nineteenth century)*

10. *Africa – textile; printed (twentieth century)*

11

1. *Africa – textile; printed (twentieth century)*

2. *Africa – textile; printed (nineteenth century)*

3. *France – wood; carved (nineteenth century)*

4. *Russia – wood; chip carved (nineteenth century)*

5. *Russia – wood; carved (nineteenth century)*

6. *Egypt – pottery; painted (3000 BC)*

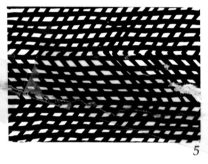

7. *Bulgaria – pottery; impressed (tenth century)*

8. *Africa – textile; printed (nineteenth century)*

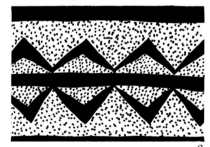

9. *Hungary – wood; wax inlay (nineteenth century)*

10. *Russia – wood; carved (nineteenth century)*

1

2

3

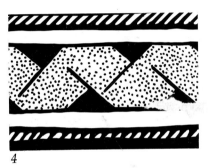

4

5

6

7

8

9

1. *Turkey – pottery; slip painted (eleventh century)*

2. *Java – textile; wax batik (nineteenth century)*

3. *England – pottery; slip painted (seventeenth century)*

4. *Italy – pottery; sgraffito (eighteenth century?)*

5. *Germany – pottery; sgraffito (eighteenth century)*

6. *Africa – textile; printed (nineteenth century)*

7. *Cyprus – pottery; slip painted (eight century BC)*

8. *Anatolia – pottery; slip painted (second century BC)*

9. *Cyprus – pottery; slip painted (date ?)*

1. Czechoslovakia – textile; woven (nineteenth century)

1

2. Czechoslovakia – textile; woven (nineteenth century)

2

3. Africa – textile; woven (nineteenth century)

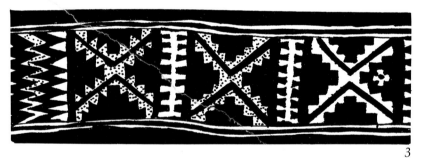

3

4. Czechoslovakia – textile; woven (nineteenth century)

4

1. *America – textile; patchwork (nineteenth century)*

1

1. *Poland – pottery; slip trailed (nineteenth century)*

2. *Turkey - pottery; slip trailed (5000 BC)*

3. *France – pottery; slip trailed (fourth century)*

4. *Yugoslavia – pottery; slip painted (nineteenth century)*

5. *Holland – pottery; slip painted (nineteenth century)*

1

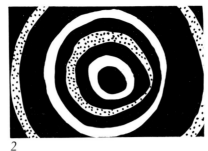

2

1. *France – pottery; slip trailed (fourth century)*

2. *England – pottery; slip trailed (nineteenth century)*

3

4

3. *Lithuania – wood; carved (nineteenth century)*

4. *England – parchment; illuminated (sixth century)*

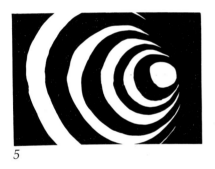

5

6

5. *England – pottery; slip trailed (nineteenth century)*

6. *America, pre-European – pottery; incised (seventeenth century)*

7

8

7. *Turkey – pottery; painted (sixteenth century)*

8. *Ireland – parchment; illuminated (eighth century)*

9

10

9. *England – parchment; illuminated (sixth century)*

10. *China – pottery; oxide painted (2000 BC)*

Introduction to circles

A circle is a closed plane curve, every point of which is equidistant from a given fixed point, the centre.

Circles are special – stand in a circle of stones and you have magic powers – dancing in a circle – holding hands in a circle – circles have long been thought of as possessing unseen powers. Of all the pattern forms circles are, at one and the same time, the most complete, the most dynamic, the most meaningful and the most satisfactory.

We think of wheels, discs, spheres, spirals, coils and all circle-related forms as being complete, self contained and full of energy. Circles are especially exciting, perhaps more than any other pattern form, because they seem to draw inspiration from, and influence, the way we live. Swinging a ball on the end of a piece of string, holding a post while at the same time walking round it and dragging a foot, skipping, the gurgle of water going down a sink, dropping a stone into a pond – these are all circle making activities.

In many folk and tribal societies the circle has symbolic significance. Life is sometimes seen as being a circle; the world is described as a sphere within a sphere; the sun is thought of as being a golden disc; and so on. And then again, ask a child to draw a face and he will almost certainly draw dots within a circle. Many primitive societies think of god, the world, humanity and everything in and around the universe as somehow or the other being capable of expression by a single circle.

Circles are exciting because, of all the pattern forms, they can be drawn and repeated with precision. Spike the point of a compass down on to a piece of paper, swing the leg around, and you have a perfect circle. Then again, once the circle has been drawn, the compass radius can be stepped off around the circumference to make a six pointed star. Once drawn, circles can be blocked in so as to make discs; shaded and graded from side to side to give the illusion of a three-dimensional spherical form; drawn one within another so as to express turning movement – the pattern and design combinations of circles are endless.

The repeated use of the compass to produce a network of intersecting circles is one of the most exciting and popular methods of making patterns. Have a look through the circle section and see how folk and tribal craftsmen have traditionally always enjoyed building circle based patterns, designs and motifs, such as moons and stars, flowers and rosettes, twists and spirals, wheels and whorls. There are chipcarved roundels on chests and beams; American folk artists found unique expression in the drawing of circle based hex-stars, and potters have always considered the circle to be central to their craft. So we could go on, listing metal workers, fabric printers and illustrators. Perhaps it is enough to say that circle related pattern forms are uniquely beautiful.

1. Switzerland – pottery; trailed slip (nineteenth century)

2. Poland – paper; papercut (nineteenth century)

3. Oceania – wood; carved and painted (nineteenth century)

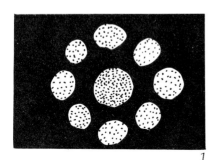

1

2

3

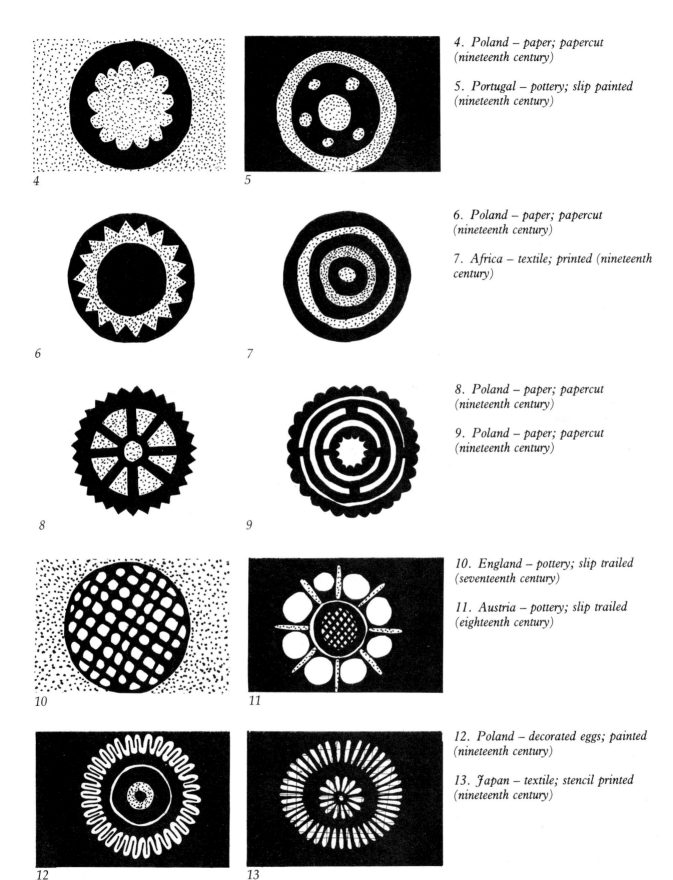

4. *Poland – paper; papercut (nineteenth century)*

5. *Portugal – pottery; slip painted (nineteenth century)*

6. *Poland – paper; papercut (nineteenth century)*

7. *Africa – textile; printed (nineteenth century)*

8. *Poland – paper; papercut (nineteenth century)*

9. *Poland – paper; papercut (nineteenth century)*

10. *England – pottery; slip trailed (seventeenth century)*

11. *Austria – pottery; slip trailed (eighteenth century)*

12. *Poland – decorated eggs; painted (nineteenth century)*

13. *Japan – textile; stencil printed (nineteenth century)*

19

1. *Hungary – wood; inlay (nineteenth century)*

2. *America – metalware; painted tin (eighteenth century)*

 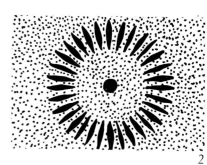

3. *America – wall; stencilled plaster (eighteenth century)*

4. *America – furniture; painted wood (eighteenth century)*

5. *England – pottery; slip trailed (nineteenth century)*

6. *America – wall; stencilled (nineteenth century)*

7. *America – furniture; painted wood (eighteenth century)*

8. *America – furniture; painted wood (nineteenth century)*

9. *America – textile; embroidered (nineteenth century)*

10. *America – textile; embroidered (eighteenth century)*

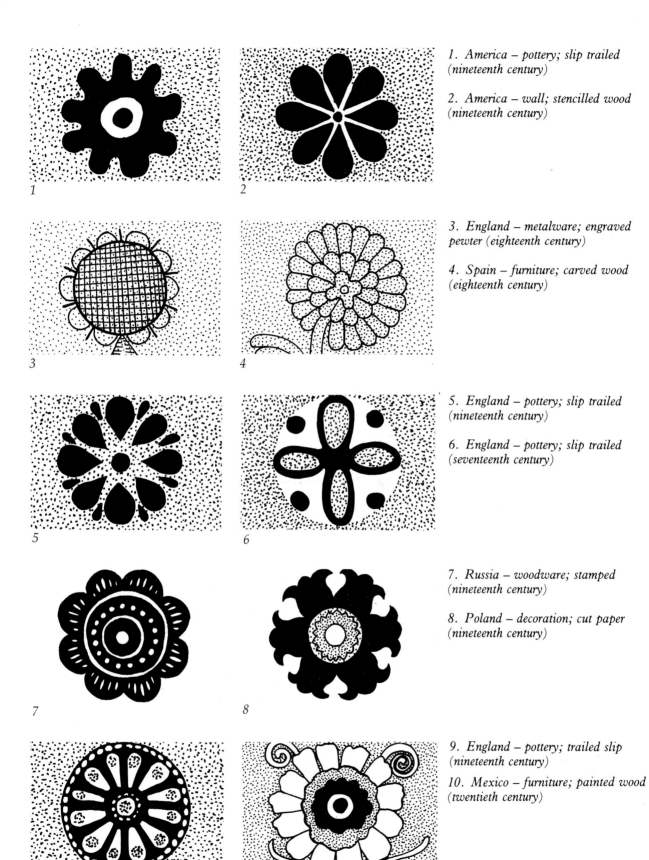

1. America – pottery; slip trailed (nineteenth century)

2. America – wall; stencilled wood (nineteenth century)

3. England – metalware; engraved pewter (eighteenth century)

4. Spain – furniture; carved wood (eighteenth century)

5. England – pottery; slip trailed (nineteenth century)

6. England – pottery; slip trailed (seventeenth century)

7. Russia – woodware; stamped (nineteenth century)

8. Poland – decoration; cut paper (nineteenth century)

9. England – pottery; trailed slip (nineteenth century)

10. Mexico – furniture; painted wood (twentieth century)

21

1. *Mexico – beadwork; appliqué (twentieth century)*

2. *Mexico – pottery; painted (twentieth century)*

3. *America – wood; carved (nineteenth century)*

4. *Italy – wood; carved (eighteenth century)*

5. *England – wood; carved and painted (eighteenth century)*

1. *Sicily – wood; carved (nineteenth century)*

2. *Switzerland – wood; painted (eighteenth century)*

3. *England – wood; carved and painted (eighteenth century ?)*

4. *Mexico – textile; appliqué (twentieth century)*

5. *Sweden – wood; painted (nineteenth century)*

1. *America – wood; painted (nineteenth century)*

2. *America – metal; tip punch (nineteenth century)*

3. *America – wood; painted (nineteenth century)*

4. *America – wood; painted (nineteenth century)*

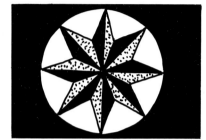

5. *America – wood; painted (nineteenth century)*

6. *America – wood; painted (nineteenth century)*

7. *America – wood; incised and painted (nineteenth century)*

8. *America – wood; painted (nineteenth century)*

9. *Sweden – wood; press-printed (nineteenth century)*

10. *America – textile; patchwork (nineteenth century)*

1. America – wood; incised and painted (nineteenth century)

1

2. America – textile; patchwork (nineteenth century)

2

1. *Iceland – metal; pierced (eighteenth century)*

2. *Iceland – metal; pierced (eighteenth century)*

1

2

3. *Iceland – wood; carved (eighteenth century)*

3

4. *Sweden – wood; carved (seventeenth century)*

5. *Iceland – metal; pierced (eighteenth century)*

4

5

1. *Sweden – wood; carved (nineteenth century)*

2. *Denmark – metal; wire (tenth century)*

3. *England – parchment; illuminated (sixth century ?)*

4. *Sweden – wood; carved (nineteenth century)*

5. *England – parchment; illuminated (eighth century ?)*

Luton Sixth Form College
Library

27

Introduction to entwined forms

An entwined form is twisted, coiled or convoluted, to give a knot, to interweave shapes or to twine them together.

In many folk and tribal societies the entwined, or interlaced pattern form is considered to be so special that the use of such patterns and designs is limited to objects and items that have to do with religion and magic.

Entwined pattern forms are best characterised by examples found on Viking carvings, on Irish and English illuminated manuscripts, on early American 'hex' paintings, and on North European chip-carved kitchen wares. One of the oldest and most beautiful of all the entwined 'magic knot' forms is that made of two or three loops interwoven and contained by a circle. Many entwined motifs are of special interest because the interlaced ribbon-like bands appear to weave in and out, under and over, in an endless confusion of strands. On closer inspection it can be seen that such designs are neither confused, nor are they made up of a multitude of strands, but rather, the one, two or three band designs are highly structured looped forms that have no ending. Such pattern forms, referred to as 'the endless knot' or the 'magic knot', took on a different meaning in the eighteenth and nineteenth centuries, when they became known as 'true-love knots' – the analogy being that like the knot, love has no ending.

The multi-stranded, love-knot, magic knot form is often found to be compass worked and geometrical in structure. Entwined pattern forms can commonly be found on items as far apart in time and space as fourth century Swedish stonework, on fifteenth and sixteenth century Swiss chests, on eighteenth and nineteenth century Scandinavian and Icelandic wood wares, and so on. In nearly every instance where entwined and magic knots were used, it was because it was believed they offered protection against the devil, ill-fortune and the evil eye.

If you are inspired by entwined forms and want to search out more designs, then look to English church bench-end carvings, and to designs on seventeenth and eighteenth century salt boxes, chests and cradles.

1. Bulagria – wood; poker work
(nineteenth century)

2. England – parchment; illuminated
(eighth century ?)

3. England – parchment; illuminated
(eighth century ?)

1

2

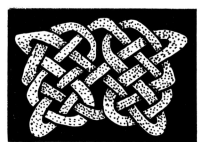

3

4

1. *France – wood; carved (fifteenth century)*

1

2. *Sweden – wood; carved (eighteenth century)*

2

3. *England – parchment; illuminated (seventh century ?)*

4. *Iceland – wood; carved (eighteenth century)*

3

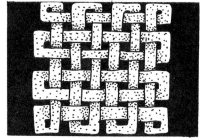

4

1. *Iceland – wood; carved (eighteenth century)*

2. *Switzerland – wood; carved (sixteenth century)*

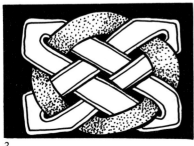

3. *Iceland – wood; carved (eighteenth century)*

4. *England – pottery; slip painted (nineteenth century)*

1. Germany – wood; painted (nineteenth century)

1

2. Norway – wood; carved and pierced (nineteenth century)

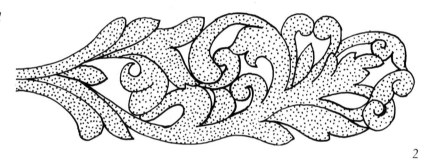

2

3. Hungary – pottery; painted slip (nineteenth century)

3

4. England – wood; carved (seventeenth century)

5. England – wood; carved (eighteenth century)

4

5

1. *Sweden – textile; embroidery (nineteenth century)*

2. *Sardinia – pottery; painted (nineteenth century)*

3. *Germany – wood; carved (fifteenth century)*

4. *Germany – wood; carved (fifteenth century)*

1. England – parchment; painted and illuminated (seventh century)

1

2. England – parchment; painted and illuminated (seventh century)

2

3. England - parchment; painted and illuminated (seventh century)

3

4. England – parchment; painted and illuminated (seventh century)

4

5. England – parchment; painted and illuminated (seventh century)

5

1. England – parchment; dyed, painted and illuminated (seventh century ?)

1

1. *Sweden – textile; embroidery*
(nineteenth century)

1

2. *England – wood; painted*
(nineteenth century)

3. *Germany – metal; cast and painted*
(nineteenth century)

4. *Java – textile; batik (nineteenth*
century)

2

3

4

1. Sweden – plaster, wall; painted (nineteenth century)

1

Introduction to plant forms

A plant form is based on a green, living terrestrial organism, such as a tree, shrub, leaf, or flower.

Garlands and flowers, leaves and rosettes, vines, tendrils, shoots, blooms, sepals and petals – craftsmen and artists have long drawn inspiration from these natural plant forms.

Textiles are a particularly rich source of plant inspired patterns. You will find white leaf-and-flower embroideries on linen, coloured flower and vine embroideries on clothes and furnishings, and so on. Pottery is another wonderful source of plant patterns and motifs, with forms variously being plant-like in shape, that is with handles, spouts and knobs looking like branches, twisted vines, buds and flower heads, or with surfaces being decorated with stylised, flat painted plant inspired imagery.

In woodwork, that is with painted woodwork and with carving, plant forms are extremely common. Structures are variously plant shaped, that is a detail might be, say, carved in the round so as to realistically resemble a plant; flat wood might be decorated with painted imagery, such as a picture of flowers, leaves and vines; or a detail might be carved in the round with abstracted plant forms. And so we could continue, looking at plant inspired forms on textiles, stone, wood, metalwork, paper, jewellery, and all the crafts in between.

We are surrounded with such a bewildering number of plant inspired patterns – much of it stylised – that we have come to see it without recognising it as being originally plant inspired. Of all the many exciting plant forms, I think the best of all are the 'flower-in-a-vase' tulip and carnation patterns and motifs. In the context of folk and tribal decoration, such forms are popular, widespread and easy to recognise. Motifs of this character can be found on just about everything from sixteenth and seventeenth wood carvings, right through to eighteenth and nineteenth century textiles, painted woodwork, metalwork and papercuts.

The painted forms, especially as they occur on early American painted dower chests, are uniquely vigorous and exciting. In the early American folk art context, tulip heads reached enormous proportions and were embellished with dot-and-dash surrounds and bordered with zigzags – really beautiful! Such works were characterised by their use of raw primary colours, by the bold naive images and by the use of unrestrained border decorations.

1. America – wall; stencilled plaster (nineteenth century)

2. America – furniture; painted wood (nineteenth century)

3. England – metalware; painted tin (nineteenth century)

1

2

3

4

5

4. *America – pottery; trailed slipware (eighteenth century)*

5. *England – furniture; stencilled wood (nineteenth century)*

6

7

6. *Italy – pottery; painted (nineteenth century)*

7. *America – pottery; sgraffito (nineteenth century)*

8

9

8. *America – pottery; sgraffito (ninteenth century)*

9. *Spain – textile; embroidered (nineteenth century)*

10

11

10. *Spain – textile; embroidered (nineteenth century)*

11. *Hungary – wood; wax inlay (ninteenth century)*

12

13

12. *Poland – papercut; folded and cut (nineteenth century)*

13. *Czechoslovakia – textile; embroidered (ninteenth century)*

1. *Africa– textile; printed (twentieth century)*

2. *Africa – textile; printed (twentieth century)*

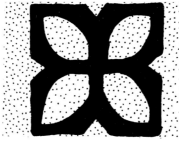

3. *America – pottery; sgraffito (nineteenth century)*

4. *America – paper; printed (nineteenth century)*

5. *Sweden – textile; embroidered (nineteenth century)*

1. *Germany – wood, furniture; painted (ninteenth century)*

2. *Sweden – textile; embroidered (nineteenth century)*

3. *Japan – textile; stencilled (nineteenth century)*

4. *America – tinware; painted (nineteenth century)*

5. *America – tinware; painted (nineteenth century)*

6. *Japan – textile; stencilled (nineteenth century)*

1. *China – paper; papercut (twentieth century)*

2. *Norway – wood; painted (nineteenth century)*

3. *America – textile; stencilled (nineteenth century)*

4. *Java – textile; wax batik (twentieth century)*

5. *America – textile; embroidered (twentieth century)*

1. *America – pottery; sgraffito (nineteenth century)*

2. *America – textile; appliqué (nineteenth century)*

3. *Poland – textile; embroidered (nineteenth century)*

4. *Poland – wood; painted (nineteenth century)*

1. Poland – paper; papercut
(nineteenth century)

1

2. Sweden – architectural; painted
(nineteenth century)

3. Denmark – textile; embroidered
(nineteenth century)

2

3

1

1. *America – tin; painted (nineteenth century)*

2. *America – wood, furniture; painted (nineteenth century)*

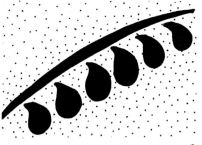

1

2

3. *Switzerland – paper; papercut (nineteenth century)*

3

4. *America – textile; appliqué (ninteenth century)*

5. *Sweden – textile; embroidery (nineteenth century)*

4

5

6. *Switzerland – paper; papercut (nineteenth century)*

6

Lytham Sixth Form College
Library

1

Introduction to animal forms

An animal form is based on any living organism having voluntary movement, such as birds, fishes, beasts, insects and man.

Animal inspired forms play an important part in western folk and tribal craft decoration. There are all manner of fabulous monsters; strange fishy-hybrid creatures; birds and beasts and finally, of course, there are any number of patterns, designs and motifs that draw inspiration from man.

Basically, animal inspired pattern forms can be divided into two groups. On the one hand there are all the designs and motifs that have to do with religion and cults, and on the other there are all the patterns and motifs that simply set out to naturalistically illustrate man and animals. Many of the naturalistic motifs are of great interest, especially when they show men, women and children at work and play. Certainly it could be said that the historical details of costume and activity often outweigh all interest of pattern and form but then again, figure groups and arrangements are in themselves pattern making.

Some of the bird forms are especially interesting – cocks, doves, eagles and the like. The cockerel form is perhaps unique because it occurs in countries as far apart as, Italy, Austria, Sweden, America, Africa, China and India. The roof-top cock is commonly, and traditionally, found on spires, crosses and barns. Supposedly, cocks are religious symbols that have to do with Christ, repentance and atonement – but why, I wonder, are they found in India and China?

If you are searching for exciting animal designs, then you can't do better than look to all the fabled birds and beasts seen in European folk art – on wood, pottery, metalwork and textiles. There are animals and beasts on rugs and hangings; serpents and mythical sea creatures on German, Swiss and English carvings; fabled horse-like creatures on Swedish carvings, and so I could continue.

If you are looking for complex, stylised monstrous creature forms, then, best of all, are the fabled beasts and monsters, the wonderfully vigorous and bolds dragons, as seen on Viking, Swedish, Norwegian and Icelandic wood carvings. There are dragon-like forms that adorn the outside of churches; dragon designs on boxes, beds and boats; dragon-horse heads on drinking bowls – all carved in bold, swirling convoluted detail.

Just about every country, period and culture favours a particular type of imaginary beast and they are well worth searching out.

1. America – wood, furniture; painted (nineteenth century)

2. Switzerland – paper; papercuts (nineteenth century)

3. Japan – textile; stencil printed (nineteenth century)

1

2

3

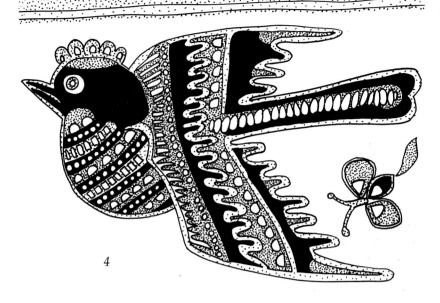

4

5. Japan – textile; stencil printed (nineteenth century)

5

1. *America – metal; cut and pierced*
(nineteenth century)

2. *England – pottery; painted slip*
(eighteenth century)

3. *France – pottery; painted*
(nineteenth century)

4. *Poland – pottery; painted*
(nineteenth century)

5. *Mexico – textile; woven (nineteenth
century)*

6. *Holland – textile; embroidery*
(nineteenth century)

7. *Poland – paper; papercut*
(nineteenth century)

8. *America – textile; appliqué*
(nineteenth century)

9. *Switzerland – paper; papercut*
(nineteenth century)

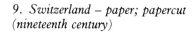

1. *America – wood; painted (nineteenth century)*

2. *China – paper; papercut (twentieth century)*

3. *Java – textile; batik (nineteenth century)*

4. *England – pottery; slip painted (nineteenth century)*

5. *America – wood; carved and painted (nineteenth century)*

6. *Japan – textile; stencil printed (nineteenth century)*

1. *America – paper; painted watercolour (eighteenth century)*

2. *America – wood; painted (eighteenth century)*

3. *Italy – pottery; painted (eighteenth century?)*

4. *Hungary – wood; wax inlay (ninteenth century)*

5. *Spain – paper; printed and colour washed (seventeenth century)*

1. Sweden – canvas, wall hanging; painted (nineteenth century)

2. Java – skin, leather; cut, pierced and painted (nineteenth century)

1. *America – wood, furniture; painted (nineteenth century)*

1

2. *America – wood, furniture; painted (nineteenth century)*

3. *Sweden – textile; woven (nineteenth century)*

2

3

4. *Mexico – pottery; painted slip and sgraffito (twentieth century)*

5. *Switzerland – pottery; slip trailed (eighteenth century)*

6. *Sweden – textile; woven (nineteenth century)*

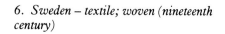

5

4

6

1

2

1. *Russia – wood; painted (nineteenth century)*

2. *Switzerland – paper; papercut (nineteenth century)*

3

4

3. *Poland – textile; woven (nineteenth century)*

4. *Germany – pottery; slip painted and sgraffito (nineteenth century)*

5. *Switzerland – paper; papercut (nineteenth century)*

5

1. America – wood, furniture; painted (*nineteenth century*)

2. Germany – textile; embroidery (*eighteenth century*)

3. Mexico – metal; incised (*nineteenth century*)

4. Sweden – textile; woven (*nineteenth century*)

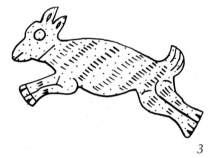 

5. America – wood; painted (*nineteenth century*)

6. Switzerland – wood; incised (*eighteenth century*)

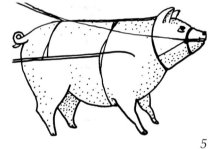 

7. Luxembourg – parchment; painted (*seventh century*)

1. *Switzerland – pottery; painted (nineteenth century)*

2. *America – wood; cut and painted (nineteenth century)*

3. *Iceland – wood, furniture; carved (seventeenth century)*

4. *Japan – textile; stencil (nineteenth century)*

5. *Africa – textile; drawn (nineteenth century)*

6. *Java – textile; batik (twentieth century)*

Introduction to borders

A border is a design or ornamental strip around the edge, or rim of a form, to give emphasis.

Border designs, patterns and motifs are special in that they include forms from all the other sections. A border might be made up of linear forms, circles, plant motifs, animal related designs, running twined patterns or, indeed, any number of combinations. The simplest way to think of a border, or a margin, is as a decorative band or strip that variously divides, contains or limits some other portion of the design. So, for example, a border might run round the rim of a pot, or it might split an area vertically, horizontally or obliquely, or it might frame and contain a special motif, so as to give emphasis. Of course if the objective is to do no more than separate two decorative elements, then a plain band or a blank space may well fulfil its decorative purpose without further development.

It is always important to ensure that the border relates carefully to the area that it contains and/or the edges of the object that is being decorated. In order to present a successful border decoration it is necessary to know at the outset its limits, such as its length, breadth, number of corners or angles, and the symmetry. Once limits have been set, then the border might contain anything from a series of thin line frames, or a row of embellished circles, through to a twined or plaited multi-stranded form, a running naturalistic leaf and vine design, or whatever. Decide at the outset just how much 'movement' you want the border to contain. Depending upon the context, a single line might be sufficient, or then again you might want to go for a a more elaborate zigzag, say one enriched with dots and dashes.

Zigzags, or wavelike border designs are particularly exciting in that they can be thought of as a potential stem or branch line, that is to say, they are capable of being easily extended and developed. In folk and tribal designs, the zigzag, the twined knot and the running vine are the most commonly used pattern forms. Have a look at the various border designs, and see how the classifications naturally tend to overlap and evolve, with oblique lines becoming zigzags, zigzags becoming vines, linked circles becoming dynamic rolling forms, and so on.

Of all the pattern and motif forms, borders are uniquely exciting, in that the field of design and the pattern and motif combinations are of infinite extent.

1. Poland – textile; embroidery (nineteenth century)

2. Japan – textile; printed (nineteenth century)

3. Iceland – wood, furniture; carved (nineteenth century)

1

2

3

4. *Russia – textile; woven (nineteenth century)*

5. *Russia – textile; woven (twentieth century)*

6. *Russia – textile; woven (nineteenth century)*

7. *Iran – textile; woven (nineteenth century)*

8. *Romania – textile; woven (nineteenth century)*

9. *Japan – textile; printed (nineteenth century)*

10. *Poland – textile; embroidery (nineteenth century)*

1. *Germany – textile; embroidery*
(nineteenth century)

2. *Poland – textile; embroidery*
(nineteenth century)

3. *America – architectural; stencil*
(nineteenth century)

4. *Poland – textile; embroidery*
(nineteenth century)

5. *America – architectural; stencil*
(nineteenth century)

6. *Czechoslovakia – pottery; painted*
(nineteenth century)

7. *Sweden – wall hanging; painted*
(nineteenth century)

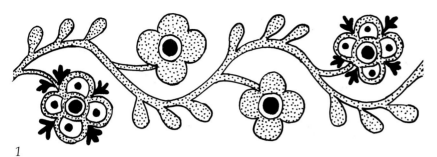

1. *Czechoslovakia – textile; embroidery (nineteenth century)*

2. *Java – textile; batik (twentieth century)*

3. *Spain – textile; appliqué (nineteenth century)*

4. *Germany – textile; embroidery (eighteenth century)*

5. *Spain – textile; embroidery (nineteenth century)*

1. *Russia – textile; woven (eighteenth century)*

2. *Russia – textile; woven (nineteenth century)*

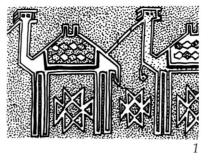

3. *America – wood, floor; stencil (nineteenth century)*

4. *Germany – wood, furniture; carved (seventeenth century)*

5. *America – wood, floor; stencil (nineteenth century)*

1. Mexico – wood; painted (twentieth century)

2. America – wood; painted (nineteenth century)

3. England – wood; carved (seventeenth century)

4. Norway – wood; carved (eighteenth century)

5. England – wood; carved (seventeenth century)

6. America – paper; papercut (nineteenth century)

1. *Sweden – wood, furniture; carved and painted (eighteenth century)*

2. *Sweden – wood; carved and painted (eighteenth century)*

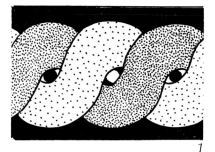
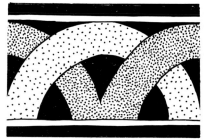

1

2

3. *Bulgaria – textile; embroidery (nineteenth century)*

3

4. *Iceland – wood; carved (nineteenth century)*

4

5. *England – wood; inlay (seventeenth century)*

5

6. *Iceland – wood; carved (nineteenth century)*

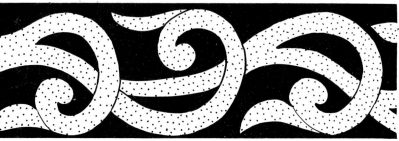

6